BARDO OF BECOMING

BARDO OF BECOMING

Poems by
Pat Williams Owen

Accents Publishing • Lexington, Kentucky • 2022

Copyright © 2022 by Pat Williams Owen
All rights reserved

Printed in the United States of America

Accents Publishing
Editor: Katerina Stoykova
Cover photo by Christine Levitt, christinealevitt@gmail.com

Library of Congress Control Number: 2022932984
ISBN: 978-1-936628-91-9
First Edition

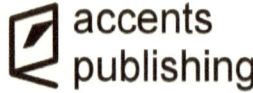

Accents Publishing is an independent press for brilliant voices. For a catalog of current and upcoming titles, please visit us on the Web at

www.accents-publishing.com

CONTENTS

Music / 1
Bardo of Becoming / 2
Summer Soft / 3
What I Want to Remember / 4
Curly Hair / 5
With My Journals Dating Back Decades / 6
The Amaryllis / 7
Saxon / 8
We Were There / 9
The New House / 10
Report Card / 12
Hiding Places / 13
Trying to Remember My Grandmother / 14
Ice Skates Hanging in the Garage / 15
Address Book / 16
Photo of Ancestors 1901 / 17
Men in Uniforms / 19
Driving to Florida Christmas Day / 20
What We Choose / 21
Returning to a Place of Early Enchantment / 22
Last Wash for the Old Car / 23
It's Clear to Me Everything's Alive and We're Part of It / 24
And the Lord Said / 25
Escaping Politics / 26
Tail End of Summer / 27
Late Friday Afternoon With Isabelle / 28
Funeral Home / 29
Annie and Her Internet Date / 30
Phone of the Unknown Dude / 31
Prodigal Son's Sister / 32
On My Screened Porch / 33
Honey / 34
Letting Go / 35
Dreaming by the Pool / 36
Skin / 37

The Spin Class / 38
We Shared a History Decades Ago / 39
Hedge / 40
Ambivalence / 41
In the Dentist Chair / 42
Billboards Shining in the Rain / 43
My Courtyard / 44
Sliders Open / 45
First Light / 46
Tropical Storm Eta / 47
Islamorada / 48
Post Pandemic / 49
The Offering / 50
What the Squirrels' Feet Know / 51
Father Harry on Vacation / 52
Extremes / 53
So Much Pain We Inflict by Being Who We Are / 55
Nature's Way / 56
View From the Back Seat / 57
Ordinary Joy / 58
Leaving / 59
When I Think I Have a Problem, I Generally Don't / 60
At the End of My Arms / 61
Impermanence / 62
Gathering After the Funeral / 63
Hawks / 64

About the Author / 65

MUSIC

It's what my frill-free childhood
needed like oxygen and it's what

my father tried to provide.
For breakfast, marching music

on the radio. He was always
whistling under his breath.

An upright piano in the living
room and to tempt me

with more lessons—musicians
appeared in our home

with trumpets displayed in a felt case,
an accordion we could try out

and then there was the clarinet
we borrowed from the school band—

all these luxuries his farm childhood
couldn't afford and now for us the best—

all stabs at nudging us out of the gray
mundane and into the exalted above.

And even now, hearing chords of piano
music, an ancient pang of guilt

that I didn't fulfill his dream.
I wish I could be for him a marching band,

tubas flashing in sunlight,
the rat a tat tat of drums.

BARDO OF BECOMING

I see me sitting on the front seat of the car with Daddy
driving, night coming on, just the two of us on the way
to Burkesville. We had snacks, a Coke and peanut butter
crackers and the question do we eat them now or later.
It was fine with him if I went ahead, he more allowing
than Mama. He was saying how the crackers became sweet
in your mouth if you held them there a long time
and let them dissolve, and I paid attention
to how that was true.

One day at about age eight, he sent me alone
to the post office to pick up a package
and I lingered to read notices of people wanted
for crimes and even now in a post office
I do the same, amazed at birth dates much later
than my own. This particular package, a special gift
for me, and I long to remember more exactly
what it was, maybe something like a kite
which we took out and flew.

And walking into school the first day of Fifth Grade,
a new school in the big city, Daddy at my side.
Keep your chin up he said, and only then the tears
almost flooding and the tightening in my throat.

Later I see my young self expounding
on something to my younger siblings
and Daddy saying, your voice is so resonant,
you will be a leader and was that the seed
that took hold?

SUMMER SOFT

Age 13 sitting on the ground
in the backyard, the world summer soft
around me, running my flat hand
over the grass thinking in some unformed
way of my virgin purity, the hard pews
of church never far from my mind.
If it's admired as beautiful,
its allure destroys it.
My aunt looking down from the porch,
what are you doing?
Of course I had no words to explain.

WHAT I WANT TO REMEMBER

What were the songs my father whistled
under his breath, what drove his heartbeat?
Isn't that tune floating now in my bloodstream?
Didn't he write a poem for me when I was just a kid
about my dreaming of a hope chest and didn't
I look at him as though he spoke a foreign
language? Mama said she's not old enough
yet, and of course I was greener than
the magnolia in the front yard,
my soul unsprouted, though it's clear
to me now I was growing toward
the strong trunk of independence
and not toward a man and a white dress.

CURLY HAIR

As a child my hair was ruler-straight.
I saw the curly-headed ones as blessed,
some special stock made them fancier,

their tops enhanced with twirls and curls,
a crown of fortune enfolds them, God's beloved,
beings with halos of favor.

And now, miraculously, late in life,
from my own top, these twirling tresses,
curving and curling, enveloping my skull

with a blessing—adornment to make royalty weep.
My inner child stunned and unbelieving, I touch
my hair shyly, stroke it just to be sure it's true.
I've gone from plain Jane to runway model.

WITH MY JOURNALS DATING BACK DECADES

I can reenter any place in time
and know it, as well as I know
the veins on my hand.

The day we arrive at the Women's
Music Festival with our red
Tourister luggage and are
picked up by a hay wagon.

I'm there breathing that familiar air.
And each time, just like now, I never
know what's coming next.

The night flying across the Atlantic
when I gave you a card surprising you
with our balloon ride over
the Serengeti Plains.

And whatever that scene appears to be
morphs into the next,
page after page, journal after
journal.

And I ask myself, has any time
been a more complete reality
than any other? What then
felt so solid and real,
changes into the next thing.
Who were those old phantoms
of myself? I have only flickers
like a changing river,
fragments of a dream.

THE AMARYLLIS

Last year a fuzzy blanket, this year an amaryllis,
gifts to encourage my girls through the gray
so you can watch for spring
my card says.

The seed for all this, the solace
I took in watching the amaryllis unfold
in the kitchen as Ellen lay dying in the living room,
checking each day for what color would emerge,
finally one morning a shocking pink,
fresh as a new day and now, years later,
finding the hyacinth burst into blossom overnight
pink and hopeful on my breakfast table.

SAXON

You were nothing but a pup
when you came to us,
kinky Airedale fur
drew hands to your lion head
for a cuddle-caress, not that you'd hold still,

but frisking, scampering away.
You knew we were untrained as you.
Leaving you in the laundry room all day
with only a radio playing, we came home
to find you trapped behind the dryer

chewing through electrical cords.
Your manners never improved much.
Visitors startled by your muscular
body hurling at them as they entered,
massive paws on their shoulders.

We settled on leashing you to a bookcase
when guests were expected. Your brute
strength could have toppled the books
but you felt contained and so were.
All the years walking the neighborhood

you straining the leash pulling me along,
neighbors saying who's walking who and the last
trip to the vet where it took two of us
to carry you to the car and on our way
the sweet smell erupting, your spirit leaving.

And the next day me lying on the rough hemp carpet
weeping, the empty house.

WE WERE THERE

If I could go back in time
any time, even a sad one,

say when we carried Saxon
into the vet's office and he died

there, we standing helpless
our arms hanging at our sides

pleading like children,
There's nothing you can do?

But we were there together
in those young bodies

in our vulnerability.

THE NEW HOUSE

In the attic I found, dusty tied with string,
packets of letters
between husband and wife,

the wife fleeing Kentucky's winters
for Florida skies—

husband home tending the family salvage
business, his days in spare parts,
the junkyard rusty and cluttered,

the harshness of his gray world contrasted
with hers, bright and sun-drenched.

I read the letters one by one,
furtive,
almost glancing over my shoulder,

words intimate in blue ink,
as individual and personal

as a fingerprint, I breathed their breath
as I read, their lives spilled out
line by line. I could almost smell them.

She felt guilty to be away, grateful.
He attempted cheer looking forward

to her return, speaking of the daffodils in bloom.
(Maybe she'll come home sooner)
By the last word of the last letter,

I merged with these ghosts, my closest companions
who once lived in these rooms,

who painted the walls a cozy brown.
I weighed trying to return the letters
to their children if I could find them,

but that would mean revealing
my guilt. Honoring their intention to preserve,

I returned the letters to their spot
in the attic where I imagine they still glow
with a soft light.

REPORT CARD

If I lick my finger and rub it
across, it would smear—
my mother's signature still intact,
pressed into the fibers
large loopy letters,
back-slanted.

Still witnessing my not-good-enough
grades, the physical evidence still
there on yellow note card,
as permanent there as in my mind
unless I add it to the shredder pile,
or drop it in the trash.

HIDING PLACES

Before we left our first home together,
    the rental house backing up to the freeway
where we made vivid pillows
    to brighten and soften the hardwood

where we paid the rent in advance
    before our trip to Europe
where we hired a teen to help us clean
    every Saturday so a shine and sheen

made everything glow
    where we worked and went to school,
juggled the kids and duties
    and now looking back,

our lives crammed full—
    vibrant, stuffed with love.
Before we left to buy our first house
    we created a time capsule to preserve

our moments there.
    Some part of us wouldn't leave, although our bodies
would occupy a different place
    where the kids would depart as inevitably as the seasons.

We hid our treasure in the ceiling of the unfinished
    basement, a dusty spot where it might
never be found. It contained a baby tooth, a traffic ticket
    and a folded note, blue-inked words spelling our lives there.

TRYING TO REMEMBER MY GRANDMOTHER

I remember a box of coconut I returned to
for another pinch of sweetness
until climbing up my sticky fingers, black ants.

I remember pictures of me at fourteen, playing jacks
on her porch, holding a kitten on the front steps.

I see her shrinking smaller
and smaller, gray hair pulled
tight into a bun on her skull,
always aggrieved in her self-sacrificing way.
Flat-chested in simple cotton dresses,
a pained smile on her lips in the family pictures.

I can bring back only one conversation.
At her sister's funeral:
You could have visited more.

ICE SKATES HANGING IN THE GARAGE

Her body, heavy with child,
pined for the skates,
if only, if only, if only
she had her body back,
she could twirl lithe and free,
reborn, chrysalis to butterfly.
Sharp blades slicing through ice,
leaving behind the sluggish, the stifling

a spray of mist in her wake.

ADDRESS BOOK

It's traveled so many miles
threadbare corners,
alphabetical tabs, frayed
and curling. Water stains
on the stitched burgundy front.

Post-it notes on the inside cover:
contact info for Jane
now in assisted living,
instructions for getting messages
from my old land line, entry
code for building.
Appliance repair references,
always trying to help my future self.

Lines crossed out with new
addresses, couples no longer
together. An astrologer, my favorite florist,
the poet whose husband tragically died,
my neighbor two moves ago,
a couple from the movie class,
therapist of an old girl friend.

Do you wince at the sight of estranged
friends? Do you scratch
out the names of people now dead?

A catalog of markings in careful blue ink.
Petroglyphs even now fading.

PHOTO OF ANCESTORS 1901

They're all dressed up for this picture-
taking day, mother and father
and five kids plus Rosa,
the orphan girl, holding
a small bouquet.
Taffeta dresses and bow ties
and suits, a tribe lined up
to be immortalized. The boys' hair
neatly combed. Mother and baby
adorned with necklaces. Care
went into this.

I'm drawn to the hands in the photo,
hers stretched across the baby,
fingers spread wide, protective,
the middle son standing,
touching the shoulder of each
parent. And the father's wide-knuckled,
folded in his lap, competent, in charge.

From this black and white world,
they gaze out, their lives as real
to them as ours are to us.
No DNA tests in those days, but
one would show a direct line
to me so I study their features
as though looking for a lost
continent. Like a migrating
bird searching for home,
I'm seeking a familiar face.

She drapes her arm casually through his,
an ownership connection, he's assured,

at ease. She's steely eyed. No one's
getting anything from her. He has
a soft tenderness around his lips,
could easily break into a smile.

The oldest boy wears knickers,
hands lie softly in his lap.
The second son stares
into the camera with a skeptical
look, *well, we'll see about this.*
A younger boy, sweet-faced
and shy, looks directly
into the camera but can't foresee
five years later
his death by drowning
in a swollen river.

MEN IN UNIFORMS

Driving onto Cape Cod late at night,
mid '70s, cops stopping us
where are you going,
and the frozen stares as we said Ptown.
Shining flashlights at the kids
sleeping in the back. Do you
have relatives there, as though
that was the only legitimate reason
to head for this gay mecca.
We were soft spoken,
diplomatic, we knew the power
of the state, the gleaming guns
in their holsters.

DRIVING TO FLORIDA CHRISTMAS DAY

Ellen wanted to stop in Nashville
to visit with her elderly cousin, Eleanor,
who would otherwise be alone.
We found her presiding in her gracious
apartment surrounded by china and antiques,
memorabilia from a lifetime of travel
with friends. Tall and large boned,
clothed in tweed, a halo of white hair,
a retired teacher with an accent
dripping with magnolia. We had planned
to take her out to eat but nothing
open Christmas Day so we ended
up in a fast-food place complete with flimsy
paper napkins.

And yet we drove away with a sense
Eleanor is fine, a steely resilience
in her fiber, just like the rest of the family.
With a toothy smile, she could face
down a class full of kids, their private
school parents, as well as the Board
of Directors. And through it all,
you could feel, she looks ultimately
to herself, and like all those I admire,
drinks from her own well.

WHAT WE CHOOSE

Foremost on her mind
her aunt should die at home
where she'd lived all her life
so Ellen checked her out
of the fluorescent-lit hospital
and drove one last trip
down winding River Road
to the old family farm
on Wolf Pen Branch
with its towering tulip poplars
where she always said her roots went down
to the center of the earth.

No expert would have advised it,
no other relative, no rational person
would have made this move
with no nursing care,
no plans in place.

Sad to confess all these decades later,
I was one of the disengaged
on the sidelines judging
How will you deal with this? and this?
but once things were set it motion,
everything worked out,
trained nurses appeared, and Ish was cared for,
she of the iron will and spunk,
drew her last breath
within the same four walls
where she was born
90 years before.

RETURNING TO A PLACE OF EARLY ENCHANTMENT

On the porch of Room 1, overlooking the Bay,
air washed clean, sunlight a benediction
on my shoulder, I'm trying to reinhabit
the time 40 years ago when we were together
in a place nearby. Will I find molecules
of us still in the air?

This place has the bright clarity of a watercolor.
Palm trees glisten with blessings, the live oaks'
long limbs drape toward the ground, constant
movement in the leaves. This enchantment
never ebbs for me.

Down below, the pool boy skims
and I watch the rowing movement
of his shoulders. Something in me
assumes that movement. All those
decades of skimming the pool
come back. I've been that body.
Long shadows stretch across the grass.

LAST WASH FOR THE OLD CAR

To honor our 30 years of caretaking
of each other and all our shiny stuff,

I take my place in line with all the others
seeking purification,

that one moment of perfection
when the grey face of the car emerges

sparkling dripping wet through the soapy steam.
Blue-shirted, brown-skinned workers,

white towels wrapped round their heads,
embrace it with rags, scrubbing

until all surfaces glow. I climb into the leather seat
one last time, fresh lemon scent surrounds me.

IT'S CLEAR TO ME EVERYTHING'S ALIVE AND WE'RE PART OF IT

The battery-operated alarm clock still ticks,
the one you gave me when I thought
the electric one would give me brain cancer.

I hear it sometimes during the night,
and here I am at Cave Hill,
your dot on the GPS.

I come here like a homing
pigeon, a heat-seeking drone.
Sunflowers and daisies for your tomb,

a celebration of your birth, the florist
knew sunflowers are right for August.
The cemetery, our most humane,

human place, where we honor life
with our flowers, our care-taking.
We take notice of the lives that have been.

Shadows streak the tombs,
an undercurrent of traffic and cicadas.
The trees breathe oxygen, a freshness

blankets the dead. Sunlight speckles
the road, a workman nods, passing.

AND THE LORD SAID

And the Lord said let there be thick fog
with herons drifting through
and let there be soft mounds of grass
with white ibis grazing.

And the Lord said let there be soft dampness
as far as the eye can see
and let there be she, soft in her skin
gazing into the fog, soft as morning.

And let there be she who has lain naked
all night in bed aware of movement
bare skin against crisp sheets.

And let there be she, aware of her mind
that she is here rather than nowhere
and let her wonder whether that's even possible.

And let there be she who rises from her chair
to begin her plan for the day.

And let there be a body to rest in
as she sits aging in place
noting what enters her eye, her mind.

ESCAPING POLITICS

I watch the egrets glide in to land—
listen hard enough to hear them
splash down in the water,
drift silent as a cloud.

Out my morning window
the world appears unmolested,
herons glide by.

On orange legs, ibis peck,
attentive to each morsel,
yummy bugs in the belly.

Fog.
The world holds its breath,
waiting.

TAIL END OF SUMMER

They're already putting out purple mums
in the nurseries, like displaying
Christmas trees before Thanksgiving.
Like everyone else, they've given up
on summer. No one goes to the pool
or puts a boat in the water,
air too heavy to breathe, spirits
sodden, weighed down by a season
past its prime.
This is a day depleted by summer
with autumn not quite here,
a forlorn, abandoned time of year,
the tail end of summer, spiritless,
it lingers. We're ready
for back to school.

LATE FRIDAY AFTERNOON WITH ISABELLE

I like picking her up at school
with a
cinnamon crunch bagel
hot-buttered and waiting
in a greasy bag in the back seat
kids pouring out the door
laughing and loud
waving at Evie lined up
for the bus, chatting
about her day, our upcoming
theater tickets
answering what a matinee is.

FUNERAL HOME

We like our undertakers in shiny shoes
unaffected by the mud.

In dark suits, creased trousers,
they stand military erect. Even as

we're stunned, blind as to what to do,
we are held aloft by their competence.

They treat us with gentleness
as though cradling a small bird.

We, the grieving, can envision dignity:
gleaming trumpets, a horse-drawn

carriage, shined boots backwards
in the stirrups.

ANNIE AND HER INTERNET DATE

My first reaction a shudder—
    old and stranger-body repulsive,
wispy hair in a thin ponytail,

trying too hard to be trendy—
    long bare arms with protruding veins,
rough-whiskered face, Adam's apple.

Sitting side by side in church,
    the unfamiliar-body tension
unspoken between them.

He takes her arm as they leave
    crossing the parking lot.
You'd have to submit to that.

PHONE OF THE UNKNOWN DUDE

We nestled it like a small bird,
three women caretaking a phone
found on the beach.
We had brushed off the sand
and tried to read the clues:
texts from *Mom* and group messages
to women with the same name.
Notices from ESPN and football sites:
a young male we concluded.
Walking around St Armand's,
we talked to it and its unknown
owner, placed it with care
in the center of our dining table,
nesting it, awaiting its ring.

PRODIGAL SON'S SISTER

Wild child flees the rules
with a move to California,
floats through parties,
mushrooms and powder.

Elder brother walks a straight path
following Father's design:
milking the cows, planting
the wheat,

while I remain in my apron
assuring everyone is fed
that there's a home
to come home to.

Wild child, out of options, drained
of health and wealth straggles home
where Father embraces the returning hero
the long-lost favored one.

Elder brother steams
resentful, unappreciated,
well aware he never got the blessing.

No one notices I'm still in the kitchen
behind the door, sharpening knives,
preparing the fatted calf.

ON MY SCREENED PORCH

Flocks of cardinals appear
intermittently. Quick actions,

nothing ponderous about a bird.
Rain blows in with the dance

of green limbs. I'm beginning
to vibrate with them. I've watched

so long I've absorbed the chlorophyll.
Isn't it ecstasy the way they move

and don't we breathe together
the same air? Leaves agitated

by the wind, the rising storm.

HONEY

The richly nuanced American word *honey*
means more than the yellow sticky stuff
for your toast. It follows "more coffee?"
in the diner. It can be touching or
demeaning depending on who says it—
condescending from an older man
intending to put you down or a genuine
sign of affection grandmother to child,
a term of endearment between lovers
as comforting as a tender laying on of hands.
It finds a compatible home in the South
where it seems to thrive in the humid air
as natural as a southern drawl.

LETTING GO

An apparition appears outside
my bedroom window.

From the second floor I look down:
—a statue, and then at first light

a slender neck and alert head, eyes
fixed on mine.

A reclining deer, keen but relaxed
taking in the morning air. I continue

to stare transfixed at this secret
world meant for no one.

I want to watch all day until another
arrives and they stand nibbling

on my rosebush and then wander away,
now indistinguishable from branches

and leaves in the nearby woods.
Fellow creature, I want to go down,

lie in the warmth where you've lain.

DREAMING BY THE POOL

Glistening in sunlight, coconut palms,
    golden in their sheen,
        wave fronds like hula skirts,

sinuous, beguiling.
    How could a being so upright
        be so seductive?

I understand
    they're breathing sunlight
        directly into their cells.

My monkey body climbs
    the smooth trunk, primate
        limbs wrapped around—

inching up, and at the top
    I bite and tear the crisp green stalk.
        We sway free and easy.

SKIN

When young I disdained
old skin like mine,
scaly like the belly of a fish
a translucent shine.

I thought something wrong
with old people,
those defective creatures,
they could have done better.

Also the flab, how could they be
so undisciplined? They just need
more effort, motivation.
So young was I, the expert.

THE SPIN CLASS

The room dark, music pounding
flashing neon, extreme exertion
moves us out of ordinary mind.

He must have died this way
fully alive,   engaged—
doing what he loved most.

He was not in a spin class
but biking on a concrete street where a body
can spin, like a Frisbee, out of control.

Surely he never knew what happened—
the two tons of crushing steel
barreling from behind.

I love you, Jack—I whisper,
in love with his vibrant aliveness
his wholesome goodness.

Now merging with the bike, I become
him in this all-out effort
sweat-drenched, panting.

WE SHARED A HISTORY DECADES AGO

Now she's reappeared, careful
on her walker.

Her fall, this time
at the museum,

instead of down the steps
vacuuming, shouting

at her husband's lies.
She was so glad to see me

in the church pew, me guilty
for not checking on her.

I'd already turned away
from her unsteady gait,

trying to distance myself
from the vulnerable,

a well I fear falling into,
drowning.

HEDGE

I want to be Mary Oliver
whose poem is chosen for the back
of the Memorial Service bulletin
to be read by the grieving,
savored,
taken home, saved in a drawer,
a hedge against abandonment,
suffering.

AMBIVALENCE

Some part of me wants to say
come get me

I'm ripe, ready,
done enough solitary

for a lifetime,
so ready to turn to someone

comfortable driving the car.
Startling how fast

my independence
dissolves like butter in a hot pan,

surprising even me.
But a needling doubt

plagues me, I'll never
be happy beating my wings

against a glass jar.

IN THE DENTIST CHAIR

A close eye to detail, the dental hygienist
leans over me, hands in my mouth,
attending, probing. This intimacy
flashes to monkeys grooming, combing,
picking out fleas. What to do with the tongue,
that most instinctive of instruments?
I will it to stay out of the way
but it shames me by nudging around
touching whatever's near. Our faces inches
apart, enlarged pores on her nose, black
hair up her nostrils. I can smell her
cinnamon mouthwash.

BILLBOARDS SHINING IN THE RAIN

Traffic lined up at stoplights,
billboards shining in the rain.
The temple still there on the corner,
laughing preschoolers inside.

Stores still selling their stuff,
all the things I bought over the years,
none of which mattered much.
Nothing of me remains

or maybe I'm part of all that's here.
Shopping carts in the Kroger lot,
people on endless errands.
It all means something

    or it doesn't.

MY COURTYARD

Drenched from the downpour, tropical plants,
bromeliads and hibiscus shine in the rain,

rooted, stoic. Sweet jasmine drapes over
the seated Buddha gazing at his clasped palms.

Pots of orchids, lavender, pink and white,
hang from the fence, thriving somehow

despite my neglect. Textured brown
mulch mimics a forest floor.

This lush world is overseen by a towering
magnolia, glossy leaves dotted with white

blossoms, votive candles of worship.
Rain still drips from the eaves.

I'm dry on the sheltered bench
breathing in the still-damp air.

SLIDERS OPEN

Socked in with tropical storm Eta,
non-stop squalls for the next 24 hours.
I have the sliders open so I can hear
gushing in the gutters. Rain
blowing in, splattering the white tile.
I know how it would feel on my bare
feet. Part of me would like to be out
feeling the tempest on my body
but judgment says stay safe inside.
We're so enveloped in this gale
it's hard to imagine
you could fly above it,
look down on it like a distant dream.
Life ghostly hushed today,
we're holding our breath for what comes next,
not only the deluge but the election.
Now no golfers in bright shirts,
no grounds crew on their riding mowers.
Even the birds have disappeared, except for
a few flecks of white ibis
misty on a distant mound.

FIRST LIGHT

I sit where I always sit
looking east over the golf course.
A soft fog settles over tufted grass,
grey-lavender clouds reflected
in the canal, a slight waver
on the surface of the water.

It rained last night I learn
when I go out for the *Times*,
water standing in the drive,
plastic-wrapped paper dripping
as I pick it up.

I tell myself, look at the world,
grow from it. The 10,000 joys,
the 10,000 sorrows. Half the sky clear
with a slice of moon, the other
half cloud-ridden, a watercolor wash.
Water shimmers, a limpkin strides by.

TROPICAL STORM ETA

Even the day after,
the world is gray and sodden,

subdued. Still haunting my mind,
yesterday's torrential rain,

battering wind, screeching
tornado warnings.

I didn't venture outside all day.

The air now so silent, shamed at yesterday's
violence. Brings back tantrums

of my own. What were the spirits thinking
to become so enraged? We can only take

a deep breath of relief. Now and then,
a tentative bird calls.

ISLAMORADA

Clouds drift over, dream-like,
lush richness in the sway of the palms
undercurrent of mourning doves.
The very air seems to call for a rum drink
with a tiny umbrella. Hemingway breathes
in the wings.

And wouldn't you know, every day
at 5:00, at the library next door,
the cat lady with a plastic sheet
to kneel on, brings food
and water for the multitude
of waiting cats, tabbies and calicos,
black and white.

And we wonder what she does
when she's not feeding cats,
she of the long gray braids,
flowered skirt skimming
her ankles, jangling silver bracelets.
Work in the library?
Care for the pet parrot
which sometimes rides
on her shoulder? She could
hardly be separated
from the scene without ripping
the fabric.

POST PANDEMIC

In my almost dream
I was a green plant
still nestling underground
in safe damp darkness
not quite ready to emerge
needing just a little more time
crouching quietly, cocooning,
conserving forces to bud forth
ready to greet the broad vast sky.

THE OFFERING

My neighbor places beside my door
a page from her coloring book.
a rabbit in soft pencil,
green and brown.
She colors to fill
the long days and nights
of the pandemic. I don't tape
it to the fridge but prop it up
in the kitchen along with the notes
and cards I want to hold onto
for a while, pieces of paper
I can't quite bring myself
to throw away, my own silent
support system on my countertop.
Possibly, after last light,
the bunny escapes my kitchen
and hops off into a grassy
field of enchantment,
returns by first light,
safely ensconced with my other treasures.

WHAT THE SQUIRRELS' FEET KNOW

The tree beside our porch bears
all we hang on it,
wind chimes, a basket
of red blossomed begonias,
but its bare branches
with spare leaves and its algae-
covered trunk speak of old age,
illness. It will bear these burdens
now, but not forever.

As much as we speak of saving it,
I fear the tree is an empty shell,
a façade, decay
at its core. Any Buddhist
can tell you resisting what is,
brings certain pain. I wonder
if the squirrels' feet detect an echoing
hollow husk.

We're awaiting the diagnosis
of the arborist, all family members
pacing the waiting room.

FATHER HARRY ON VACATION

His legs, white and bare,
usually secluded behind black robes,
broadcast their nakedness.
But he shines with a scrubbed wholesomeness
fresh from the shower, new clothes
from a just-opened box, crisp blue shirt,
creased khaki shorts.

His face shines with an Irish priest
glow, his smile beatific.
A perpetual shimmer surrounds
him. He bestows on all he meets
praise, enchantment and his full attention.

He's always someone's guest
and forever in glamour spots
at peak season. Everyone
yearns to bathe in his aura,
bask in the warmth of that sun.

EXTREMES

Excess was her specialty. Too much
food, drink, attitude. Passionate in idolizing
celebrity and if her hero was a woman
athlete, all the better. She loved to pose
with her *best friend* and post
for the world to see. Everything
in her life a superlative, the best
or the worst. Fiercely loyal,
she celebrated the birthday
of her pets years after their deaths.

She delighted in wheelies
on ice and preferred riding her chopper
with no helmet,
the better to feel the breeze
in her hair. She had pride
in all she touched: the best
boat, car, yard, neighbors.
Under a tough façade,
she was quick to weep
over a friend's misfortune.

When she got sick she believed
if only she got a new fridge
that would get things cold enough
everything would be ok,
and if she could get chicken noodle
soup hot enough, she would be strong
again.

But the most important
thing you need to know,
as I stood on the sidelines

safe and careful,
and too often passing judgment,
she laughed and cried,
got too many sunburns,
and in the end
had no regrets.

SO MUCH PAIN WE INFLICT BY BEING WHO WE ARE

She could never please her mother
who was, after all, French, and had
her standards. No matter how hard
the American daughter tried,
her facial structure would never
allow her to sound truly French.
She spent a lifetime trying
to understand why she wasn't worthy
of love. Rocks rubbing against rocks.

They say each generation is an over-
reaction to the last one.
Inevitable bruising in this pendulum swing,
heads knocking against heads.
I heard a priest say,
be quick to forgive
unintended consequences.

NATURE'S WAY

Her death no surprise in some way.
A china doll of porcelain bones,
she ate a few bites of lettuce
and called it lunch. No amount
of coiffing her carefully colored
hair could hide her fragility.
You knew one fall would shatter
her. I feared for her aging body
and for my own.

Sometimes I wonder if car crashes
are just nature's way to purge people
on their way out anyway,
like a big cat waiting for the slowest
antelope, the weakened ready
to be taken. We choose, in some way,
don't we, our deaths? It would take
only a slight swerve of the wheel.

VIEW FROM THE BACK SEAT

So strange seeing intimacies
from the back seat

like being dropped unseen
into someone's bedroom.

Neck massages for the driver,
driver's hand reaching

over to the passenger seat for some
unseen tenderness,

maybe just a hand on a knee.
A moment of gentle affection,

shining in its simplicity.

ORDINARY JOY

Delighted to get in the shower
each day, one moment in time

of soapy scrubbed
perfection. I get out dripping,

step fresh onto the blue
fluffy bath mat now imprinted

with my wet footprint, and towel
dry, ready for clean clothes.

My purification exercise,
a relinquishing of the past,

redemption for a new day.
This must be something like

forgiveness, a spotless beginning.

LEAVING

It's better to be the leaver than the left,
more green shoots of new growth,
remembering my wedding dress
hanging on my bedroom door
me departing into my new life
the emptiness of the left behind.

I haven't had much experience
as the left behind
always being the one to leave
cutting all ties, getting in the car and gone
Trip-tik maps beside me on the seat,
this the slant I choose to savor.

Now the young are flying off, winging
into new vistas and I find myself on the porch
staring out on an almost dead tree. Just today
a hawk swept down into my yard, lingered
a few moments and then soared away. I still
hear it calling to me from the high trees.
A song is playing in my head, to breathe,
you must leave.

WHEN I THINK I HAVE A PROBLEM, I GENERALLY DON'T

This was the day of the lost earring,
my favorites I've worn every day
for a decade, silver beaten discs
from Oaxaca, which I've prized
like they're breath itself. Last night
one fell off the table, and no
amount of feeling under the bed
turned up anything but dust.
During the night, reliving
Ellen's irretrievably lost Mikimoto
ring bouncing on the kitchen
floor, I feared this too, like Ellen
and her ring, would be forever gone.

After my all-night restless plotting how
to replace it, next morning, lugging
the heavy terra cotta lamp, then emptying
and scooting the Mexican table, down
on hands and knees, sliding my palm
over layers of lint, there it was,
glowing like a treasure.

AT THE END OF MY ARMS

Sometimes I look at my hands
old friends
and see my mother
or a stranger
mute beings
somehow attached to me
blindly in my service
poor things.

I study them in wonder
like something you'd see in a museum
safely behind glass.
Skin loose like crepe now
but still the fingers spread wide
strength and competence.
And no matter how faithfully
they've served me
part of me knows
their warranty will expire.

And then I see them
with something like love
as you'd look at your aging dog
limping with that bad hip
knowing
that last visit to the vet
is coming soon.

IMPERMANENCE

Inside the house they're tearing down
frequent bouquets of daisies
we picked up at the grocery store
and arranged in a blue earthenware pitcher
that at other times held home-brewed iced tea.
The daisies fresh in their bright white and yellow
glowed on the kitchen table
and we refreshed them over the week
with long draws of water from the kitchen tap.
These daisies if you pressed them
between thumb and index finger would bruise
and leave on your hand a fine yellow powder
that would remain until you rinsed them
under a cold stream at the sink.

GATHERING AFTER THE FUNERAL

Someday, the time may come
when your family and friends
are sitting at round tables
eating a nice lunch while photos
of your life flash
on the screen, slides of your young
self, smiling and vibrant,
throbbing alive.

Conversations around the table
about upcoming vacations
and plans for the afternoon.
From time to time someone
looks up at the screen,
but then down at their plate,
hearing the clink of silverware,
spreading butter on a soft roll.

HAWKS

My daughter thinks hawks are loved ones
come back to protect her and who knows,
maybe someday I'll be soaring high above
the tall trees looking down, but today we're
walking together in the park and as we pass
the glistening magnolia and holly trees, I
do not say *that's what I wanted to plant*
for the twins until the idea was vetoed
as too messy. And I feel good about
holding back, not treading on hurtful ground,
practicing for next time, and for the time
after that, until I grow closer to the goodness
I can only imagine.

ABOUT THE AUTHOR

Pat Owen went from the left brain world of legal publishing to the right brain of world of poetry. Her work has appeared in *Gulf Stream Literary Magazine, Louisville Review* and several anthologies. She was a finalist in the Atlantic Review International Poetry Competition. She was an award winner in the Chautauqua Writer's Center 2020 Literary Arts Contest. *Sheila-Na-Gig online* published her poem "Hawk" in its Summer 2021 edition. Her debut poetry collection, *Crossing the Sky Bridge* was published by Larkspur Press in 2016. Her second collection, *Orion's Belt at the End of the Drive* was published by Accents Publishing in 2019.

www.ingramcontent.com/pod-product-compliance
Lightning Source LLC
Chambersburg PA
CBHW030200100526
44592CB00009B/374